His Words are in Red

Adoria Luster

His Words are in Red

ISBN-13: 978-0615731742 (Breathed Ink)
ISBN-10: 0615731740

Printed in the United States of America
© 2013 by Breathed Ink
www.hiswordsareinred.blogspot.com

adoria.luster

Breathed Ink
2271 Saratoga
Oceanside, California 92054

Contents

Acknowledgements

First, I give all thanks, honor, and glory to God for the grace and longsuffering He provided me as I strove to obey Him in completing this work.

I also thank my husband Donnie—the man of my dreams and my brother in the Lord who is and has been a constant source of support and encouragement throughout this endeavor. I love you, honey.

A special thank you to my children, Jasmine, Precyous, and Jeremiah, for believing that I could write this book and for always cheering, "Mommy, you can do it!" May you all walk before the Lord all the days of your lives. I love you.

Lastly, but certainly not least, I want to thank my friend Mae. The Word of God says, "Most men will proclaim each his own goodness, but who can find a faithful man?" I have found one in you. Love you, always.

Forward

This book came to me in a dream given by God. He gave me the title, *His Words Are in Red*, and He revealed that I was the author. The clarity to write this work continued to unfold over time. I worked on this book for over twenty years, which to me seemed excessively long. However, I recognize that His thoughts and ways are higher than my own, and it has taken this journey for me to appreciate and submit my own desires and thoughts to His Word. The title of the book speaks to His authority and dominion over all, especially His people. God made provision for us by sending His only begotten son Jesus, who shed His blood for the sins of the world. The title *His Words Are in Red* denotes His supreme power and right.

I have written this book to instruct, inspire, encourage, provoke, and chasten the people of God into heeding the voice of God and answering Him with the fullness of our hearts. Each of us is ultimately responsible for our obedience to God. I believe that none of us dares to think that we could stand before a Holy God and give excuses as to why we could not follow Him! I believe that when we stand before God, it will be without any pretense and without the ability to hide our true selves from Him. We are and will be completely visible and transparent before Him.

In keeping with the purpose of this book I have not included scripture references to the Bible in the text. As His people, we are directed by His Word, "Beloved, do not believe every spirit, but test the spirits, whether they are of God; because many false prophets have gone out into the world." (1

John 4:1 for example) We with the guidance of His Holy Spirit must determine the accuracy of this work and thereby grow in Him. All teachings and writings must be examined by His Word. I pray that God would allow each of us to see ourselves clearly within the light of His Word and to know Him. I ask that He would grant us repentance when we need it, and guide us into truth, for He is truth. I pray that God would open our hearts, enlighten our minds, and give us the wisdom and strength to walk before Him until that day when we dwell with Him forever.

This book is a call for holiness unto God, for separation from the world, and for us to discern our hearts truly in the light of His Word. It can be likened to a trumpet sounding the call, "Prepare ye the way of the Lord; make His way straight." I pray that His people hear His voice and reply with unity, "Here I am, Lord; may it be unto me according to your Word."

Chapter 1
God's Word

For the believer, the Bible is not a collection of ancient tales with a viable option of how the world and man began. The Bible is more than a book kept in a place of honor in the home whose purpose is to record the births and deaths of family members. It is more than a book by which one swears to tell the truth in a court of law. The Bible is more than a collection of ethical or moral examples of life or occasional verses to inspire. For the believer, the Bible is God's Words. The Bible tells us all things that pertain to life and godliness. The Bible is the communication of God's thoughts, heart, and ways. The Bible is God-breathed. Holy men wrote the Bible as God's Holy Spirit moved them to do so.

The Bible is the communication of God's thoughts, heart, and ways.

It is impossible to express with words the depth, worth, and profound nature of God's Word. His Words are spirit and they are life. For the believer, this truth is revealed within us as we meditate on His Word. His Word stirs our inward parts with faith and feeds our hearts. His Word nourishes our spirits, renews our souls, and breathes life into our mortal bodies. His Word anchors our souls and instructs our paths. Through His Word, we attain life, and it sustains our lives from day to day. In Him and through Him we live, move, and have our being. The very core of who we are is joined to God through His Word. He is the vine and we are the branches.

In the beginning was the Word, and the Word was with God, and the Word was God. He was in the beginning with God. All things were make through Him and without Him nothing was made that was made. In Him was life; and the life was the light of men. The Word was made flesh, and dwelt among us, and we beheld His glory, the glory as of the only begotten of the Father, full of grace and truth. That which was from the beginning, which we have heard, which we have seen with our eyes, which we have looked upon and our hands have handled, concerning the Word of God. There is not a time when the Word of God was not present. God's Word is God.

This passage of scripture recorded in the Gospel of John declares Jesus Christ as the essential Word, as our source of personal wisdom, and as the embodiment of the power of God. Jesus, in union with God, created the worlds and all that is contained in them. Jesus came in the likeness of man to save man's soul, and His Words and deeds declared Him as God.

There is no name higher than the name of Jesus. There is no other name given whereby men can be saved. Yet God has magnified His Word above the name of Jesus. In this, God declares the authority of His Word. His Word is to be esteemed above all.

God upholds all things by the Word of His power. God's Word is the spirit of life for those who believe in Him. It is the foundation of our salvation and the cornerstone of our faith. God's Word is the path to truth and the way to eternal life. To know God's Word is to know God. God has revealed Himself through His Word.

The men and women of the Bible knew the voice of God. They believed that God spoke to men and moved them to act on His behalf according to the words He spoke to them. This was evident in the lives of Abraham, Moses, Zacharias, Mary,

Saul, numerous kings, angels, and many of His people. To us, the Words of God are written in the Bible. God, who at various times and in various ways spoke to the fathers through the prophets, has, in these last days, spoken to us through His Son, whom He has appointed heir of all things, through who also He made the worlds.

God speaks to His people today through His Word. God does not change. He is the same yesterday, today, and forever. God continues to speak to us through various ways, and His written Word confirms what He says.

For unto us a Child is born, unto us a Son is given; and the government will be upon His shoulder. His name will be called Wonderful, Counselor, Mighty God, Everlasting Father, and Prince of Peace. Jesus is the fulfillment of the Word of God as a promise to the world. His Word says, "Heaven and earth shall pass away, but My words will by no means pass away." All that God has spoken is fulfilled in Jesus. Moreover, Jesus said, "It is finished." All that God has spoken is established and proven. All of history declares the truth of His existence, and His Word establishes all history and determines all of the future.

According to the scriptures, God has spoken to His people in different ways. In many of His teachings, Jesus said, "You have heard it said…." He said this because, at that time in history, all that was known of God was that which was taught by the priests, the Pharisees, the Sanhedrin, and other learned men of that day.

John the Baptist preached that the Kingdom of God was at hand. John said, "I did not know Him, but He who sent me to baptize with water said to me, 'Upon whom you see the Spirit descending, and remaining on Him, this is He who baptizes with the Holy Spirit'."

Moreover, it is written that John said, "Him whom God has sent speaks the Word of God." Jesus fulfilled the Word of God spoken to John and the prophecies foretold by the prophets. Through these scriptures of truth, we acknowledge that God spoke to John and through John.

Today, we have the written Word as the fulfillment of the Word of God. The Bible says, "Lo, I come in the volume of the book; it is written of me, to do thy will, O God." The written Word of God reveals not only who God is, but it reveals the fulfillment of His promises as well. It reveals Christ Jesus. As Christians, we often look at the scriptures to find ourselves. However, He says, "You search the scriptures, for in them you think you have eternal life, and these are they which testify of Me." Scripture was not given to humankind so that we could find ourselves, but that we might find Him and know Him. The Word of God is not written about you and me; it is written about Jesus, our glorious Lord and God! The only way to know God is through His Word. When we begin to know Him through His Word, we will begin to know who we are in Him—that we are the righteousness of God in Christ Jesus.

Confessing and receiving Jesus as our Lord and Savior gives us access to God the Father, it also gives us the right to know God. The veil that covered our eyes is removed so that we can understand His Word. These acts do not give us the knowledge of God or His Word. We must also repent, which is to turn from the direction in which we were going and walk in newness of mind, spirit, and heart, according to His Word. Then we pursue the knowledge of God, which comes through prayerful mediation and study of His Word.

Proverbs states: My son, if you receive my Words, and treasure my commands within you, so that you incline your ear to wisdom, and apply your heart to understanding, yes, if you cry out for discernment, and lift up your voice for understanding, if you seek for her as silver, and search for her as hidden treasures, then you will understand the fear of the Lord and find the knowledge of God. For the Lord gives wisdom, and out of His mouth comes understanding.

Those who are called by His name and are sealed by His Spirit understand the relevance of God's Word in their walk with Him. It was asked of the Lord, "How is it that You will manifest Yourself to us and not to the world?"

Jesus answered and said, "If anyone loves Me, he will keep My Word; and My Father will love him, and We will come to him and make Our home with him. He who does not love Me does not keep My Words; and the Word which you hear is not Mine but the Father's who sent Me."

Beloved, God's Word is His gift to us; it is our life and light as we walk with Him on the earth. His Word is given that we may know Him and His will. Through His Word, we find Him.

God's Word is the active element that lives within us and makes us one with Him. He is the vine and we are the branches. It is through obedience to His Word that we are transformed into His image. Herein is the mystery of the Gentiles: Christ in us, the hope of glory. His Word is quick and alive in us. If we will obey His Word, we will truly be living epistles to be read of all men. This is the will of God.

The Bible is not for anyone's private interpretation, and God has warned that no man should add to it or delete from what He has said in His Word. Holy men of God wrote as they were moved by His Holy Spirit. The Word of God is living, powerful, and sharper than any two-edged sword. It pierces even to the division of soul and spirit, and of the joints and marrow, and it is a discerner of the thoughts and intents of the heart. There is no creature hidden from His sight, but all things are naked and open to the eyes of Him to whom we must give account. We can put on pretense for those around us, but in the light of His Word, we are all exposed. As Christians, we should want our deeds to be exposed whether they are good or evil.

In the light of His Word, the perfect law of liberty, the true intention and genuine deliberation of our hearts and our souls is revealed. Yes, the Word of God is the power of God, for He has declared that it would be so, and not for the glory of man, but for His own glory. His Word is settled forever in heaven. The entirety of His Word is truth, and every one of His righteous judgments endures forever.

The Word of God is pure, holy, just, and true. His precepts are perfect. His statues give life to the hearers and strength to their souls. His Word makes a heart merry. We come to know this first because it is written, and then through obedience to His Word we bear fruit as witnesses. We experience its benefits. Bless the Lord, O my soul and forget not all His benefits:

- The eyes of the Lord are on the righteous, and His ears are open to their cries.
- Who can forgive sin, but God alone?
- God is our rock, our shield, and our fortress.
- He will set them on high because they have known His name. They shall call upon Him and He will answer them.
- His covenant He will not break, nor alter the Word that has gone out of His lips.
- He sent His Word to heal them and deliver them from their destruction.
- Fear not, for He has redeemed us. He has called us by our name. We are His.
- The Lord is our Helper; whom shall we fear? What can man do to us?
- With long life, He will satisfy them and show them His salvation.

The Word of God is right, proven and established. God is faithful. We know and have confidence in these truths because He has spoken them, and because they are written in His Word forever. Oh, that men would give thanks to the Lord for His goodness and His wonderful works to the children of men.

God's Word

Chapter 2
Have Faith in God

The Bible asks, "When the son of man comes, will He find faith on the earth?" He will certainly not find faith until we, as His people, come into the mature knowledge of faith and its purpose. Faith is simplistic. Faith is what we believe. It is our conviction of belief in the authenticity of God. Faith is the confidence that activates, generates, and propels our thoughts and actions.

Faith is being sure of what we hope for and certain of what we do not see.

Faith is not wishful or positive thinking. Faith is the complete assurance within our hearts that God is who He says He is. Faith is a necessary ingredient that requires every part of us, including our hearts, minds, and will. The existence of God is not a fallacy, a myth, or a fairytale, yet it takes faith to believe in Him.

God created the heavens, earth, and all that is in them. He created two great lights, the sun to light the earth by day and the moon to light the earth by night. He created the stars as well. He created every creature of the sea and every living thing that moves upon the earth. He created humanity in His own image, male and female. By faith, we believe this is the creation of the world and that it is God's workmanship.

Faith without corresponding action is useless. We cannot touch it, we cannot provide physical proof of its existence, and it is foolishness to the world. The Bible says that faith is the substance of things hoped for and the evidence of things not seen. Another translation says faith is being sure of what we hope for and certain of what we do not see. With that in mind, what is it that we hope for? What are we sure of that we do not see? God! We do not see God, and yet we believe. The same is true of salvation! We do not see salvation, and yet, by faith, we are certain that we have been born again, and by this same faith, we work out our salvation with fear and trembling. Though we have never seen Him, we love Him, and even though we do not see Him now, we believe in Him and are filled with inexpressible and glorious joy, for we are receiving the goal of our faith—the salvation of our souls and eternal life!

Faith within itself is useless. For the believer, faith is the reason for our expression of obedience in what we say and do. We pray because we believe in God and in His ability to hear us, and we believe it is His desire that we do so. We walk before Him in a manner that conveys our belief in the commandments He has given us. We conduct ourselves based on our belief in the genuineness of God. We believe in God because He alone gave His life so that we may have life. We live by what we believe God desires, requires, and commands of us, for the just shall live by faith.

Faith is honest and basic. What matters is not how great our faith is but how great God is in His faithfulness toward us who believe. Faith is not positive thinking or positive confessions. Faith is not the repetition of words or a mantra that forces our desires to materialize. Faith requires trust, because trust is an act of faith. As we mature and learn more about God, we experience His faithfulness, and we base our trust on our relationship with Him. We trust and have assurance in God because He is constant. God never changes. His Word is sure, and there is no variance or shadow of turning in Him. God is trustworthy. We can rely completely on Him and trust what He has said is true. Our faith can rest in Him surely.

We have been taught that faith comes by hearing, and hearing comes by the Word of God. This does not mean that if we recite any scripture frequently enough, our faith will increase simply from hearing the scripture repeatedly. We must understand that this scripture is not talking about how often one vocalizes the words of his or her desires and hears them.

Prior to the verse above, the Word says, "Lord, who has believed our report?" Both of these scriptures are referring to the preaching of the gospel that was not obeyed by God's people (the Jews), and that there would be a people who would have faith in Him upon hearing the gospel of Christ (Gentile Christians). Hearing and believing God's Word made us who were not a people a chosen people, a royal priesthood, and a holy nation. Therefore, by our faith, we were made the people of God.

Our faith in God is the source of all spiritual warfare. In the beginning, Satan asked Eve, "Has God indeed said?" Adam and Eve knew what God had declared, and yet when questioned and confronted about their belief, their faith was shaken. A similar question was posed to Jesus when Satan tempted Him, inquiring, "If you are the Son of God...." Yet Jesus, being mature in His faith and confident in His belief, responded, "It is written...." When our confidence and full assurance rests in God's Word, we experience victory in spiritual warfare, for the battle is the Lord's. He defends His people as they walk in obedience to His Word.

When we, as the body of Christ, respond in times of spiritual warfare the same way our Lord did—by stating what is written, and by living according to His Word—then we will partake of the same victory over temptation that our Lord experienced. Then He will indeed find faith on the earth. The entire reason for spiritual warfare is to determine our faith in God's Word.

That is why He said, "Fight the good fight of faith laying hold of eternal life." The goal of our faith is the salvation of our souls.

Like most Christians, I have read and heard numerous teachings on faith, but God alone revealed to me the truth of faith. As I walked through the valley of the shadow of death and through many trials of life, I attempted to use the formulas of faith taught to me. I prayed the sufficient amount of time. I confessed only the right words. I refused to acknowledge or speak that which was not of the said faith to which I was confessing. I even refused natural knowledge. I only spoke those words that were reflective of what I believed. I spoke daily to the mountain of my circumstance and commanded the circumstance to be removed. I found no resolve, no change, and I came to no hope. The mountain did not move.

I could not escape the one truth that God is incapable of failing or lying. Therefore, I concluded that there was a flaw either in me or in the teaching of faith that I had believed and embraced wholeheartedly. The emptiness in these formulas forced me to search anew. In that search, I found truth. The God of truth revealed to me that He is not in the formula, He is not in the words, and He is not in our righteousness.

God told Elijah to go out and stand on the mountain before the Lord. The Lord passed by and a great and strong wind tore into the mountains and broke the rocks in pieces before the Lord, but the Lord was not in the wind; and after the wind an earthquake, but the Lord was not in the earthquake; and after the earthquake a fire, but the Lord was not in the fire; and after the fire a still small voice, a delicate whispering voice.

We must adhere only to the voice of God, and not believe in formulas, steps, signs, wonders, or the lying powers of any person who tells us of our past or our future. We must not believe those who suggest that the promise of God is with stipulations or conditions, and that by our own actions we can attain the promises of God. Our faith must be in His Word and His Spirit.

God revealed that I have no power to move mountains unless He has declared it. I have no power to stretch forth my hand to heal unless He guides me to do so, and if I run where He has not told me to go, I run in vain. If I speak what He has not said, my words are useless. He made known a truth that I believe we must value above all else: "It is in Him that we live, move, and have our being."

He uncovered the truth of my heart, which had deceived me, for my faith was not in Him but in my own desires and my own self-righteousness. The Bible says that you ask and do not receive because you ask amiss so that you may spend it on your pleasures. My heart and faith were not in Him, but in the formula. My faith was in my words, in my actions, and in my diligence. My faith was not in Him or in His Word.

As I embraced the truth of God's Word concerning faith, I found fulfillment in all things. I learned to accept whatever state I am in and whatever set of circumstances I have, for my faith is not in the things nor in the circumstances, but in God.

As I walk by faith and not by sight, only the Word of God moves me. I learned that my riches are in Him, and that even though each of us walks a different path, salvation is the goal of our faith. I am learning what the true riches of Christ are, and I am committed to striving toward Him in faith. Our faith must be firmly rooted in Him and through Him alone. Have faith in God, brethren!

Chapter 3
The Heart of God

There is so much information about the heart of God. I imagine the topic to be one of the most popular of all subjects written about God. Perhaps it is because of our desire to understand the essence of God. We are blessed because He has made Himself known to us through Jesus Christ, for God, who cannot lie and does not change, has declared that Jesus is the express image of His person. Through Jesus, God demonstrates His heart. God's Word says, "Out of the abundance of the heart, the mouth speaks," which shows that God's heart is clear through the manifestation of Jesus our Lord. God and His Word are one. There is no separation or division between them. They agree. Let us look at some of the ways that God's heart is revealed to those who believe.

Each of us must learn to know God's heart by reading His Word.

The heart of God makes provision for us through Jesus. In Jesus, God's thoughts, plans, and purposes are established. The Word of God tells us that Jesus is the way, the truth, and the life. No one comes to the Father except through Him. The only way to comprehend and appreciate the heart of God is through Jesus. Each of us must learn to know God's heart by His Word. Any doctrine that describes God's heart as anything other than what Jesus demonstrated when He walked the earth is a lie! Any premise or philosophy that bolsters man's goodness or worth prior to the blood of Jesus covering his sins or continuing in His righteousness is fraudulent and will lead to death.

God's heart determined the way that we would come to Him and the way that we must walk with Him. He purposed our path. He decided and created truth, for His Word is truth and He demonstrated truth in Jesus. Moreover, in Him alone is truth. His Word tells us that Jesus is the door; all others are thieves and robbers. The thief does not come except to steal, to kill, and to destroy. This thief is not the devil, as many have been taught. The thief is men or women who are imposters of Christ, and as such, they do not care for the sheep. Jesus is the Good Shepherd who gives His life for the sheep. He cherishes and cares for His own. God made provision for His people to be reconciled to Him through Jesus. This is the heart of God.

Jesus said that His sheep hear His voice, the voice of truth that God has declared as His, and any other voice that does not come from the heart of God should not be followed. We hear and know the voice of God through the Words and life of Christ.

We are a peculiar people in that we can know the thoughts and intents of the heart of God that He has chosen to reveal through Jesus Christ. The Bible states and we acknowledge that God is love. God manifested His great love toward us by sending His only begotten Son into the world that through Him, we might live and have everlasting life. This is love: not that we love God, but that He loved us and sent Jesus to be a substitute for our sins. Oh, what manner of love the Father has given unto us that we might be called the sons of God!

The Bible asks, "Who can separate us from the love of Christ. Can tribulation, or distress, or persecution, or famine, or nakedness, or peril, or sword? For I am persuaded that neither death nor life, nor angels nor principalities nor powers, nor things present nor things to come, nor height, nor depth, nor any other created thing, shall be able to separate us from the love of God which is in Christ Jesus our Lord."

God's love is everlasting, and He proves it through Jesus, who lives forever. Because He continues forever, He has an unchangeable priesthood. Therefore, He is also able to save those who come to God through Him. He lives to make intercession for us. The heart of God is love. Love is in the heart of God, and it is His will that we would not be separated from Him.

The scripture tells the story of how Jesus was walking throughout Galilee one day when a leper came up to Him, knelt down before Jesus and said, "If you are willing, You can make me clean." Lepers were outcast, unclean, and not permitted in the city gates.

Jesus said, "I am willing; be cleansed." The Heart of God says "I am willing!" The Word tells us that immediately the leprosy left the man and he was cleansed. Jesus demonstrated God's Heart to the leper. God's Heart does not require steps and formulas for man to prove he is worthy. We are not worthy. God knows what is in us, for He is our Creator. The Bible tells us that God saw that the wickedness of man was great in the earth, and that the intent of the thoughts of man's heart was only evil continually.

This poor leper acknowledged God's superiority over him and his unworthy state by bowing before God and imploring Him to see his condition and have mercy on him. The Word tells us that Jesus was moved with compassion. The heart of God is merciful and full of compassion.

Another example of God's heart revealed is the story of a certain man who had two sons. The younger of them said to his father, "Give to me the portion of goods that falls to me." Therefore, the father divided his livelihood and gave to his sons.

The younger son journeyed to a far country and there wasted his possessions with wasteful living. He spent all his money and eventually became so hungry that he desired to eat the food for the swine, and no one gave him anything. Then he came to himself and decided to go back to his father's house.

This son knew his actions were against his father's will. He was raised in his father's house. This brings to my mind thoughts of so many Christians I know who have left the house of our Father in their hearts and are now hungry. The Bible tells us that when this son was still far off in the distance, his father saw him and had compassion on him. His father ran and fell on his neck and kissed him. The son said, "Father, I have sinned against heaven and before you, and I am no longer worthy to be called your son." Nevertheless, the father said to his servants, "Bring out the best robe and put it on him, and put a ring on his hand and sandals on his feet. Bring the fatted calf here and kill it, and let us eat and be merry, for this my son was dead and is alive again; he was lost and is found." They rejoiced.

It is important to note what the father did not say in this scripture. He did not say to his son, "I know you have sinned." This parable demonstrates that God's love and compassion for us is not contingent upon our performance. God knows when our hearts are sorrowful, and He is looking for us to return to His embrace. God desires that His people return to Him with sorrowful hearts when we have strayed from Him. In this parable, we see that God does not forsake man, but man forsakes God when he is enticed and led astray by the lust of his heart. It is God's heart to forgive and restore. God is full of mercy and kindness, and He is longsuffering. He is tenderhearted and forgiving to those who cry out to Him with earnest and sincere hearts.

The eldest son in this parable remained comfortably at home in his father's house, yet he failed to rejoice at his brother's return. The father said to this son, "Everything I have is yours. Nevertheless, it is right to rejoice, for your brother was dead, and is alive again." This scripture speaks volumes about the intent of God's heart toward those who remain in fellowship with Him. He said that everything He has is ours! Nevertheless, He wants us to maintain a heart that is pleased for our brethren's reconciliation and desirous of God's will for all. This is the heart of God.

In another scripture, we see Jesus gathered together with many people, preaching and declaring the Words of God to them. The people brought to Him a paralytic who they carried down through the roof of the house. When Jesus saw their faith, He said to the paralytic, "Son, your sins are forgiven you." God is good, and His heart is forgiving. God sees our faith and knows our sin. He alone possesses the power to forgive and heal.

In another recording, Jesus was on the cross between two men deserving of their fate, yet He was dying for your sins and mine. Jesus was mocked, ridiculed, and scorned, yet He was sinless. He prayed, "Father, forgive them, for they do not know what they do." God knows our weaknesses, our frailty, and our vulnerability. He also knows our stubbornness, our willfulness, and our presumptuousness. He knows our nature. He knows the heart of each of us individually. He knows we are but dust, and yet still He forgives.

God tells us that godly sorrow will lead to repentance. This means that He gives us the ability to turn away from sin and toward Him. He has given us the ways and means to return to Him when we stray. In addition, He gives us strength through

His Word and Spirit to walk with Him. The goodness of God leads us to repentance. God's heart is pure.

The Bible tells us that a dispute arose between Jesus's disciples about which of them would be the greatest. Jesus questioned them, asking, "Who is greater: He who sits at the table or he who serves?" Jesus was the One among them who served. He said that he who would be greatest of us would be the servant of all. Jesus washed the feet of those who He called and taught them the ways of God. He answered when His Father called Him to serve, and He went where He was requested to go. He was born in a manger and made Himself of no reputation. He had no place to lay His head. Nevertheless, He is the express image of God's glory. Jesus is the very heart of God walking among men. He is the very heart of God within us that leads us to our Father.

In the scriptures, Jesus tells Peter that Satan had asked permission of God to sift Peter as wheat. Satan requested to harm Peter, similar to when Satan presented himself to God in the Old Testament prior to afflicting Job. God is aware of all things. His eyes are not dim, and His arm is not short. In telling this to Peter, Jesus displays God's knowledge of the wicked one and his evil doings. Jesus prayed that Peter's faith should not fail. Jesus did not say Peter would not be shaken. His prayer was that Peter's faith would not fail. Peter's faith needed to be firmly rooted in Jesus. Our faith in the unending, never-failing power of God should be steadfast, unmovable, and unshakable because of what Jesus, the very heart of God, demonstrated to us. Jesus as a High Priest at the right hand of God ever lives to make intercession for His saints. Jesus prays today that our faith would not fail when we too are sifted and shaken. His care for us is ongoing. God's heart is abiding.

The Heart of God is that we would come unto the fullness of Christ Jesus. He desires that we would come to maturity in our walk with Him. We should know the plans of God, in that He Himself gave some to be apostles, some prophets, some evangelists, and some pastors and teachers, for the equipping of the saints for the work of the ministry; for the edifying of the body of Christ, until we all come into the unity of the faith and the knowledge of the Son of God; to a perfect or mature man; to the measure of the stature of the fullness of Christ.

God has made through His gifts every provision for us to know Him and grow into maturity in Him. This is the will of God demonstrated through His Son and our Lord Jesus. Jesus answered all when asked of His disciples. He spoke to the people He ministered to in parables, but to His own disciples, He said that He revealed to them (and now us) that which had been kept secret from the foundation of the world. Christ within us is the hope of glory. God's will is that His heart would live in us.

Jesus tells us that the kingdom of heaven, meaning that place where He is King (inside of us) and where the authority of His Word is supreme (inside of us) is likened to ten virgins who took their lamps and went out to meet the bridegroom. Five were wise, and five were foolish. The five foolish virgins were not prepared with oil in their lamps at midnight when a cry was heard: "Behold, the bridegroom is coming; go out to meet him!" Oh beloved, do not allow yourself to be found foolish at that hour. For many do not know the heart of God for themselves. Many have foolishly relied on another and not in Jesus, the bosom of God. Do not allow yourself to be lulled into sleep and be found wanting through traditions of men and doctrines of demons and lies. Refuse to be one who tolerates an imitation of godliness but denies the very power of godliness. The power of God dwells within the heart of God.

Always remember, beloved, that God said that His Spirit would not always strive with man. God's heart has cried out concerning the times and the seasons, "Brethren, you have no need that I should write to you. For you yourselves know perfectly that the day of the Lord comes as a thief in the night. For when they say, peace and safety! Then sudden destruction comes upon them, as labor pains upon a pregnant woman. They shall not escape. Let not this heart be you! However, you, brethren, are not in darkness, so that this Day should overtake you as a thief. You are all sons of light and sons of the day. We are not of the night or of darkness. Therefore, let us not sleep, as others do, but let us watch and be sober. Let us look unto Jesus and know with certainty within ourselves the heart of God."

Chapter 4
The Glory of Obedience

This chapter is called the glory of obedience, for truly it brings glory to God when His people are obedient to Him. Glory is the opinion, judgment, and view of one's actions that result in praise, splendor, and honor. Obedience is comprised of the acts and deeds of willingness, compliance, submission, and/or observation of all God's requirements. Obedience for the believer requires two elements: the heart and works of faith. Obedience is our duty and obligation because of who He is and what He has done for us. Obedience is our reasonable service, not a laborious and grievous task offered as a sacrifice. The Lord does not desire that type of sacrifice, but rather, the sacrifices of God are a broken spirit and a contrite heart; these He will not despise. God has spoken His desires to His people and made known what He expects and requires. He desires that His people, who are called by His name, would humble themselves and pray, and turn from their wicked ways. He requires obedience from the heart and in the manner in which we live.

The behavior of the obedient brings glory to His Name.

The word *obedience* evokes many different responses; some are of the heart, and others are the actions we take. Our individual responses to the word *obedience* are direct indicators of our knowledge of God and of the intent of our hearts toward Him. We may be pleased with our current walk or find ourselves wanting. Some people may find that they are self-righteous, having only obedient actions while their hearts are far from God. Some may profess a sincere love for God from the heart with no obedient actions to show that love; thus, they bring no glory to God. The attitude of the heart must be motivated to obey the Word of God by growing in the knowledge of Him. With this heart of obedience, we deter our selfish nature from seeking its own glory, and we remain indebted to Him who has called us into obedience. Whether we identify with the person who has obedient actions without the love of God in his or her heart, or with the person who loves God from the heart without corresponding actions, we must humble ourselves and be obedient. Even though Jesus found Himself in the form of a man, He humbled Himself and became obedient unto death, even the death of a cross.

The behavior of the obedient brings glory to His Name. Our obedience displays our opinion of Him. God is faithful and worthy and our response is obedience. Through obedience, we display before the whole world that God's ways are perfect and that His statues for us are good. Our obedient, submitted heart demonstrates God's glory and proclaims that He is deserving of honor, splendor, and glory. Through obedience, we partake of His glory and receive within ourselves all the promises God has given to us. Obedience demonstrates His kingdom, which is righteousness, peace, and joy in His Holy Spirit. Obedience within the heart of the believer is true riches to be cultivated, protected, and treasured. For all those who practice walking as He has commanded, obedience affords the confidence of knowing He will do exactly what He has promised. God is with those who obey. They bring Him glory, and He is their joy.

Beloved, immaturity is no excuse for disobedience. As we walk with God, our knowledge and understanding of Him must increase. God expects this growth in us. His will is that we all come into the fullness of Christ through maturity. We must understand that to everyone who has the knowledge of God, more will be given, and he will have abundance; but from him who does not have, even what he has will be taken away. We cannot be content with our current knowledge of Him but desire to know more. As we mature, our knowledge of God and obedience to His Word should increase, thus bringing God glory. As Paul said, when I was a child, I spoke as a child, I understood as a child, and I thought as a child, but when I became a (wo)man, I put away childish things. With the understanding that God knows the totality of us—our thoughts, intents, and all that is in our hearts—let each of us come to maturity and walk obediently before Him, that we would bring glory to His name.

Obedience is a deliberate effort. We must set our minds on the things above and wash our minds by the water of God's Word. We must think on those things that are true, noble, just, pure, lovely, and of a good report; if there is any virtue and if there is anything praiseworthy, we must meditate on these things. We must cast down arguments and every high thing that exalts itself above the knowledge of God, bringing every thought into captivity to the obedience of Christ, and being ready to punish all disobedience when our obedience is fulfilled. We must cleanse our hearts, our hands, our thoughts, and our deeds. We must walk worthy of the vocation in which He has called us. We must press toward the upward calling of God, to be perfect even as He is perfect. Our obedience is His glory.

An obedient heart is deliberately grateful; it understands that God's grace toward those who believe is unmerited and undeserving. By grace, we are saved through faith, and that not of ourselves; it is a gift from God, not of works, lest anyone should boast. For while we were yet still dead in our trespasses and sin, Christ died for us. The appreciation of this truth and the acknowledgement of the depth of Jesus's sacrifice will result in willing obedience. When we fail to grasp who He is, and we seek not His will for us, we make life decisions based upon our own desires and wants. We fall short of the glory of God instead of walking in obedience to what He has commanded. God does not withhold any good thing from us. We must be committed to maintain fellowship with Him through obedience and knowledge of His great sacrifice.

God's plan for us is pure and simple. He desires that we walk holy and live righteously in Him. To accomplish His desire requires obedience. He tells us not to look to the left or the right, but to walk circumspectly. He tells us that there are false teachers and false prophets prepared to deceive, yet He gives us the blueprint to endure all through obedience. He says that all for His name's sake will hate us, but he that endures to the end shall be saved. Salvation is only possible through obedience. The life He has purposed for us is not without trial or testing, and if we walk in a godly manner, it will not be without some suffering. It is not a life that is to be filled with natural or earthly riches, for how can a rich man enter into the kingdom of heaven? It is not filled with the pleasures of this life and earthly joys. Yet, our life is filled with purpose, hope, and longing, and with faith and joy that our Redeemer lives. Ours is a life that has been spoken of through the ages: that God would dwell in temples not built by the hands of man but by God Himself. This promised life is only realized through obedience. Therefore, we must gird up the loins of our mind, be sober, and rest our hope fully upon the grace that is ours through the revelation of Jesus Christ. We must do this as obedient children, not conforming ourselves to the former lusts, as in our ignorance; but as he who called us is holy, we must also be holy in all our conduct. Holiness is impossible without obedience to His Word.

Without a firm foundation of the Word of God and a ready heart to receive the truths of God's Word, it is difficult if not impossible to walk in obedience. If we do not know God's Word in truth, we do not know what to obey, what to believe, or why we should submit ourselves to the disciplined life of walking in obedience with Him. If we do not maintain a prepared heart within us for why we obey, we may be obedient on occasion, but when the trials of life come our way and the deceitfulness of this world inundates us, we will not be able to endure with continuous obedience—certainly not the continuous obedience of the heart.

Jesus told us this in the parable about the sower who sowed the Word of God. Each example in the parable tells us of the condition of the soil within our hearts. Depending on the various conditions of the soil of our hearts, the Word is or is not obeyed. He told us that the devil would come and take the Word out of the heart of some who hear only; some who have no root or foundation within them would endure for a while, but during temptation would fall away. In addition, with some, the Word would be choked because of the cares, riches, and pleasures of life; these would not reach spiritual maturity. Yet, some who hear the Word would have a cultivated and prepared heart that would keep the Word and bear fruit with patience. This fruit is the glory of obedience.

My beloved, too often we are taught about obedience as it pertains to natural things, but true obedience is spiritual, for it is from the heart that we believe, and then our actions follow. The teachings about what natural objects can be obtained by formulas or conformity to concepts and manners of thinking regarding obedience are useless as it pertains to God's glory.

Teachings that declare what can be attained by the laws of God and yet fail to discern the weightier spiritual matters such as justice, righteousness, mercy, holiness, and faith, are flawed and incomplete, because none of these character traits can be acquired without an obedient heart and obedient actions toward God. An example of using the laws of God for a natural purpose without having a heart for God is when God's Word says, "Give and it shall be given unto you." This is a law of God; thus, it works just as He has declared it: If you give, it shall be given to you. The spirit of this law of giving is not for the purpose of self-gain. Did God purpose that by giving, the giver would become rich or that the poor would have enough? The spirit of this law is that the poor and those in need would have their needs met, and in obeying God's Word, the giver would be blessed as well, for it is more blessed to give than receive, which is a spiritual truth. Hence, it is imperative to know that it is impossible to bring glory to God through obedience without discerning God's Word by His Spirit. This is because the Word of God is spirit, and obedience is spiritual. Man may attempt to take from God's Word that which pleases or suits his natural purpose, yet he fails to obey the spirit in which God wills. We must not focus on the letter of the law, but instead obey God and the spirit of the law. For this will bring glory to God.

I would be remiss if I failed to speak of disobedience, for I do not wish that any would be ignorant of God's Word and thereby perish. Disobedience is to ignore and/or reject the truth of the commands and direction of God. We must not disregard God's Word for any reason. We must know that God's plan for our life is good and not evil, and that obedience is the way to salvation. Through obedience, He leads us by still waters and restores our soul. Through disobedience, we will live in defeat, despair, and torment. Narrow is the gate and difficult is the way that leads to life, and few there are who find it. Yet, wide is the way that leads to destruction, and many through disobedience are on that path. His Word says, "Do you not know that to whom you present yourselves slaves to obey, you are that one's slaves whom you obey, whether of sin to death, or of obedience leading to righteousness?" Be mindful of these words, beloved, for He wills that none would perish but that all would come to the knowledge of the truth. His Word says that He has no greater joy than to hear that His children walk in truth. Walking in truth is synonymous with obedience. Again, His Word says, "Keep the charge of the Lord thy God to walk in His ways, to keep His statutes and His commandments, and His judgments, and His testimonies, as it is written, so that you may prosper in all that you do no matter which way you turn."

As Christians, we must be aware of the consequence of disobedience. Disobedience is sin. Disobedience is rebellion against God's Word. Do not deceive yourselves or be deceived by others. Being continually disobedient to the Words of God, whether in heart or in deed, is the rejection of His Word. This will only lead to separation from God, death, and eternal damnation. This is not the will of God. He commands that we walk in obedience, and He does not make compromises with any justifications or explanations as excuses. Remember, the Lord God judges righteously, testing the mind and heart.

When I consider His ways, I am awestruck by the goodness of God in giving us the charge to bring glory to His Name through obedience. He, the author of life, has provided the method by which to convey His glory, and we are the instruments that He has chosen. I am mindful of His words to Solomon, "As for you, my son, know the God of your father, and serve Him with a perfect heart and with a willing mind; for the Lord searches all hearts, and understands all the imaginations of the thoughts; if you seek Him, He will be found of you; but if you forsake Him, He will cast you off forever." As in all things, God is just. He has set before us this day as with everyday a choice. I pray that we would choose to give Him glory through our obedience.

Chapter 5
Call Him Lord

This was the most difficult chapter to write. When I call God my Lord, I think of myself, and I ponder how He is Lord to me.

God is not only Lord of the believer; He is Lord of all.

He is truly the Lord of my life. Therefore, I begin with what I know. The Lord God is the existing one. God's Lordship did not begin with Jesus. Genesis, the first book of the Bible, starts with, "In the beginning, God...." All of our knowledge of God derives from His Word and from what He has revealed about Himself therein. All autonomy belongs to the Lord. He is completely sovereign, yet He has given His Word as His will. Regardless of what anyone believes, He said, "I am that I am," and He has displayed His power and majesty throughout history. His being is a matter of certainty for all. Since the creation of the world, all of humankind has seen His invisible attributes in the world of nature. We can understand Him, including His eternal power and Godhead, in all that He made by His spoken Word.

God is not just Lord of the believer. He is Lord of all whether in heaven, in the earth, or under the earth. For it is written, "As I live," says the Lord, "every knee shall bow to Me and every tongue shall confess to God." Everyone will give account to God. The Lord God is the Judge of the living and the dead. His Lordship is not limited to our realm. He is Lord of heaven, of earth, and of all that is under the earth. Heaven is His throne and earth is His footstool.

His Lordship was spoken at the creation of the heavens and the earth. The Lord created all that is in the earth—grass, herbs, seeds—and told the seeds to produce after their own kind. Likewise, the Lord God created the creatures of the seas and every living thing that moves on the earth and every winged bird. He blessed them and said, "Be fruitful and multiply. Then the Lord God made man in His own image and breathed life into man and made him a living soul."

After the disobedience of Adam and Eve, the Lord God displayed His goodness in that He covered their nakedness, which had become a source of shame to them now that they had sinned. In this act of kindness, the Lord declared that He is merciful, and that He is ever mindful that we are but dust. We must acknowledge that the Lord God's thoughts of us are good and not evil, and recognize that in His Lordship He retains all knowledge at all times of all things.

Some have ventured to speak as to why the Lord created all that He has. I will not do so. The Lord has not revealed His purposes for the creation of humankind; only that He is the One who created us. He has determined that we should walk before Him. We are called into the fellowship of His Son, Jesus Christ our Lord. The hour is coming, and now is, when the true worshipers will worship the Father in spirit and truth, for the Father is seeking such to worship Him. His Word identifies those who have walked in obedience to His Lordship. They are pleasing in His sight because they fulfill His will.

The Lord is omnipotent. He is all-powerful and unstoppable. There is no force in heaven, on earth, or under the earth that can stop or compete with God's will. People often pit Satan against God as if the two are equal. Satan is not equal to God. The creation cannot be compared to or compete with the

Creator. God has always existed. His existence is not contingent upon anything, whether human or spirit. God is above all.

The Lord is omnipresent. He is everywhere at once. His presence has no limitations or boundaries. The scripture declares, "Where can I go from thy presence?" There is no one, nothing, or any place hidden from the presence of the Lord.

The Lord is divine. His divinity speaks to His triune nature called the Godhead. He is the Father, the Son, and the Holy Spirit. He is the one and only true God. His Word says that we ought not to think that the Godhead is like gold, or silver, or stone, graven by art and man's device. In God's sovereignty, He determined that the fullness of the Godhead would dwell in Jesus. Through God's divine power, this same Jesus, who we call Lord, has given us all things that pertain to life and godliness, through the knowledge of Him that has called us to glory and virtue, in that He has given us Himself.

That which the Lord has promised and spoken is sure. He has confirmed by an oath two immutable things: It is impossible for God to lie, and when He could swear by no one greater, He swore by Himself. The Lord promised to provide a Savior to His people and to all people so that all would be reconciled to Him by Himself, whether things on earth or things in heaven, having made peace through the blood of His cross. "For God so loved the world that He gave His only begotten son that whosoever would believe in Him should not perish but have everlasting life". The Lord God is the author of life. As it is written, the first man Adam was made a living soul, and the last Adam was made a quickening spirit. Jesus, being perfected, became the author of salvation and eternal life to all who obey Him. Therefore, we look unto Jesus, the author and the finisher of our faith. His Word says that heaven and earth shall pass away, but His words will by no means pass away. All that God has spoken was fulfilled in Jesus, which Jesus signified when He said "It is finished" the moment before dying on the cross. All that God has spoken is established and proven in Jesus. His truth declares all of human history, and the future is determined by His Word.

The Lord God is the authority over all who believe in Jesus and have called upon His name for salvation. He provided His blood as a sacrifice substitution for our sin, and He purchased us through the shedding of His blood. His Word says that we are not our own and that we belong to Him. He is the possessor of our entire being.

The Lord Jesus is the King, and the kingdom of heaven belongs to Him. The kingdom is where the King Jesus resides in complete authority and dominion. The kingdom is the place that the Lord provides for His people to walk in victory. Our victory is in our submission and obedience to His Lordship. We are commanded to seek the kingdom of God before all else, and we are promised that it is the Father's pleasure to give us the kingdom. His kingdom is not of this world, and we gain entrance to His kingdom through many tribulations. We must walk worthy of God who calls us into His own kingdom and glory. The kingdom of God is not in word but in power. His kingdom is righteousness, peace, and joy in the Holy Spirit. The Lord said that He would give us the keys to the kingdom. The Lord is King and reigns over His kingdom, and of His kingdom there will be no end.

The Lord God is holy. His holiness sets Him apart from all gods, places, and things. He is sacred and blessed, and thus, He is to be worshipped. His Words and His Will are above all because of His holiness. The Lord told Moses to take the shoes from his feet, for even the ground where God's presence was is holy. The place where He dwells is called a holy hill in the Old

Testament, and it is also called His holy temple. His Spirit is Holy. Jesus is the Holy child. The written Word is Holy Scripture, His angels are spoken of as holy, and we are called a holy nation and a royal priesthood. Our bodies are holy temples. The beasts around His throne do not rest day or night, for they cry out "Holy, Holy, Lord God Almighty, which was and is and is to come."

Every precept, statute, and command of God is perfect. The Lord in His ultimate wisdom gave statutes, percepts, and commands whereby we must live in Him. These rules that govern our lives are established through His judgment. His Word says that the government would be upon His shoulders. He has established the statutes that He uses to judge all. When we understand the prudence of His Lordship, we then readily receive and believe what is written: "Eye has not seen, nor ear heard, nor has entered into the heart of man the things which God has prepared for those who love Him." We then embrace that His thoughts and ways are higher than our own, and His will for our lives far exceeds anything that we could ever imagine.

Throughout the Word of God are multiple accounts of men and women who, by God's Spirit, recognized the Lordship of God. The psalmist wrote, "What is man that You are mindful of him, or the son of man that You take care of him?" In another place, man cries out with an understanding of God's Lordship by asking, "Where can I go from Your Spirit? Or where can I flee from Your presence? If I ascend into the heaven, You are there; If I make my bed in hell, behold, You are there. If I take the wings of the morning and dwell in the uttermost parts of the sea, even there Your hand shall lead me, and Your right hand shall hold me. If I say surely the darkness shall fall on me, even in the night shall be light about me; indeed, the darkness shall not hide from You, but the night shines as the day; the darkness and the light are both alike to You." The Lord God is the existing one. The Lord is omnipotent and omnipresent. He alone is God, and there is no one or anything hidden from His sight.

As I mediate upon His Lordship, what more can I say? The scriptures tell us that if all the works of Jesus were written in books, there would not be enough books in the world to recount His deeds. No wonder the Israelites spoke of God with a sound that words could not articulate before God Himself gave them a name by which to call Him.

The Lord God is full of mercy and justice. He is forgiving and enacts judgment. He is longsuffering and jealous. He is the prince of peace and a man of war. He is the lamb slain before the foundation of the world, and He is the Lion of the tribe of Judah. Moreover, He is all simultaneously. He is Lord of all! Words fail to convey the magnitude of His Supreme Being. Yet, for all His majesty and splendor, He chooses to dwell within the hearts of those who distinguish Him and submit to His Lordship with their whole hearts and beings. How can we not call Him Lord?

Chapter 6
God's Holy Spirit

The Holy Spirit of God is perhaps the most misunderstood and misrepresented aspect of God within His Church.

Through the Holy Spirit, God's expression and approach are revealed to us.

Therefore, I will begin with truths recognized in His Word regarding His Holy Spirit. The Holy Spirit is God. God's Holy Spirit and God's Word are one; as such, they agree in all things. God's Holy Spirit does not act independently or in contrast with God's Word. God's Spirit does not work in mysterious ways. His Word says, "For what man knows the things of man except the spirit of the man which is in him? Even so, no one knows the things of God except the Spirit of God." Moreover, the Word tells us, "When He, the Spirit of truth, has come, He will guide you into all truth; for He will not speak on His own (authority), but whatever He hears He will speak, and He will tell you things to come." "He will glorify Me, for He will take of what is Mine and declare it to you." The Holy Spirit of God does not act autonomously. His role is in conjunction and harmony with the Word of God. The Holy Spirit leads and guides us in truth. His Word is truth. God's Spirit reveals God's Word. The Father, the Son, and the Holy Spirit are one, and all three are God.

The Bible declares that its contents are "not by the will of man; but holy men of God spoke as the Holy Spirit moved them." The Holy Spirit gives utterances from God, and all true prophecy is by Him. For no prophecy of Scripture is of any private interpretation.

The Word of God always refers to the Holy Spirit as a personalized force. In the scriptures, God's Spirit is never referred to as "it" or as a force separate from God. God's Spirit is not energy or a feeling. Although He possesses power and sometimes manifests Himself in ways that can be felt, we are not to be moved by feelings, but by the Word of God, which His Spirit unveils. The Holy Spirit characterizes God's manner to us. Through the Holy Spirit, God's expression and approach are revealed to us. We could say that God's personality is made known by His Holy Spirit. The character and personality of His Spirit is holy. An example of this is an account in the New Testament of the disciples' reaction when a village did not receive Jesus or them as they prepared to go to Jerusalem. James and John asked Jesus, "Do you want us to command fire to come down from heaven and consume them?" Jesus rebuked them and said, "You do not know what manner of Spirit you are of. For the Son of Man did not come to destroy men's lives but to save them." Many today use the Word of God without knowing the Spirit of God's Word, and in doing so, they error. Our sufficiency is from God, who also made us sufficient as ministers of the new covenant, not of the letter but of the Spirit; for the letter kills, but the Spirit gives life.

John said that which was heard we have seen with our eyes; we have looked upon it and our hands have handled it, concerning the Word of life, and that the life was manifested, and he bore witness and declared to us that eternal life was with the Father. This Word of life became flesh and dwelt amongst us. By His Spirit, His Word became flesh. This same Spirit makes known His Word to us and in us. By the Holy Spirit of God, we become living epistles as His Word is written in our hearts. Through our obedience, His Word becomes flesh in us, and all those we encounter can read His Word through the example of our lives.

God's Word says, "In Him we live, move, and have our being." This is only possible through His Holy Spirit. For the kingdom of God is not eating and drinking, but righteousness, peace, and joy in the Holy Spirit. Thus, it is impossible to walk in Christ without the instruction and guidance of His Spirit.

His Word clearly identifies that the fruits, works, acts, and deeds of God's Holy Spirit are love, joy, peace, longsuffering, gentleness, goodness, faith, meekness, and temperance. For the Spirit of God is in all goodness, righteousness, and truth. God's Spirit is referred to as the Spirit of Truth in relation to His deeds and power. He will cultivate us as we walk in His Spirit and demonstrate the fruit of the Spirit, and as we deny the lust of our flesh.

His Word tells us, "All manner of sin and blasphemy shall be forgiven unto men; but the blasphemy against the Holy Spirit shall not be forgiven." God does not take lightly evil speaking and slander against His character. The Bible tells us not to grieve the Holy Spirit. For it is by the Holy Spirit of God that we have been sealed for the day of redemption. His warning is, "Hear now, O house of David! It is a small thing for you to weary men, but will you weary my God also?" God will not always strive with man, for we are but flesh and He has numbered our days. I therefore, the prisoner of the Lord, beseech you to walk worthy of the calling with which you were called, with all lowliness and gentleness, with longsuffering, bearing with one another in love, endeavoring to keep the unity of the Spirit in the bond of peace.

The Word of God says that the gospel of Jesus Christ did not come in word only, but also in power, and in the Holy

Spirit, and in much assurance. This scripture declares that the Holy Spirit is more than power. He is all power. He is the totality of God's strength, power, and might. He is God.

God's Holy Spirit is referred to as the breath, wind, or force of God. His Spirit manifests His will and ability. His Word tells us that in the beginning, "The earth was without form and void; and darkness was on the face of the deep. And the Spirit of God was hovering over the face of the waters." God spoke, and His Word and His Spirit created all. In the conception of Jesus, Mary was told by the angel Gabriel, "The Holy Spirit will come upon you, and overshadow you; therefore, also, that Holy One who is to be born will be called the Son of God." The angel spoke God's Word, and with His Spirit, God created life. After His resurrection, Jesus appeared to His disciples. The Bible says, "He breathed on them and said to them, 'Receive the Holy Spirit'." On the Day of Pentecost, they were all in one accord in one place, and a sound came from heaven as of a rushing might wind, and it filled the whole house where they were. All who were present were filled with the Holy Spirit and began to speak with other tongues as the Spirit gave them utterance. Until this time, His disciples had not preached of Him or done any miracles in His name since the physical departure of Jesus at His ascension into heaven. In these examples, God reveals the power of His Spirit to create and give life, His life. God demonstrates His breath upon His Word through physical manifestations. Through His Word, He declared that it would be so, and His Spirit confirmed and manifested His Word. He also revealed that it is His will to dwell within the human vessels that He created.

In the Word, Jesus tells His disciples that after He departs He will send them another Comforter. This Comforter is the Holy Spirit. He calls the Holy Spirit the Spirit of Truth, and He tells them (and us) that the world cannot receive Him because the world does not see Him or know Him, but that we know Him, and that He will dwell with us and in us. The Greek word used for Spirit in this passage of scripture is *Parakletos*, which means intercessor, consoler, advocate, and comforter. Perhaps this is why Jesus said that He would send them another comforter; until this time, Jesus had been all things to His disciples. The Holy Spirit would take the place of the physical presence of Christ Jesus, the anointed Son of God. Jesus says, "When the Comforter comes, whom I shall send to you from the Father, the Spirit of Truth, who proceeds from the Father, He will testify of Me." All that the Holy Spirit speaks, reveals, and performs is of God's Word and in union with it.

His Word declares that the hour is coming, and now is, when the true worshipers will worship the Father in Spirit and truth, for the Father is seeking such to worship Him. "God is Spirit, and those who worship Him must worship in Spirit and truth." True worshipers are the complete opposite of pretenders, whether imaginary or counterfeit. Those who are not true may demonstrate the motions of worship by the lifting of hands or bowing of their knees. However, true worshipers embrace His Spirit of truth through obedience with sincerity of heart, bowing their whole lives in submission and worship before our Holy Father. God knows those who are His.

The Word tells us, "When He (the Holy Spirit) has come, He will convict the world of sin, and of righteousness, and of judgment; of sin, because they do not believe in Me (Jesus) of righteousness, because I go to my Father and you see Me no more; of judgment because the ruler of this world is judged." This is only possible by the indwelling of God's Holy Spirit within His disciples. We are His disciples, indeed, if we have been born again and baptized. When God's people walk in His

Spirit, which requires obedience to His Word, the world is convicted of sin, is reminded of the need for righteousness, and is warned of judgment. The Holy Spirit does not convict the world independently of God's church, because the church is the body of Christ. The Holy Spirit within us convicts the world of sin as we gloriously and purely demonstrate the truth of God's Word through our obedience to it. We are living epistles.

We must consider that Jesus began His ministry after the baptism of John. John bore witness to this, saying, "I saw the Spirit descending from heaven like a dove, and He remained upon Him." His Word also says, "For He whom God has sent speaks the Words of God, for God does not give the Spirit by measure." Jesus walked on the earth with the full measure of God's Spirit. Jesus prayed that His Father would give us His Spirit to be with us and in us. His prayer is "that they all may be one, as You, Father, are in Me, and I in You; that they also may be one in Us, and that the world may believe that You sent Me." Today, we His disciples have been born from above and sealed by His Spirit. His Holy Spirit dwells within us. His Word instructs, "That good thing which was committed to you, keep by the Holy Spirit who dwells in us."

Moreover, He has given of His Spirit through gifts to men. His Word says that there are diversities of gifts, but the same Spirit of God gave them all. There are differences of ministries, but the same Lord. In addition, there are diversities of activities, but the same God works in all. The Holy Spirit is the One who works all these gifts, and He distributes them to each of us individually as He wills. As His body, we are many members, yet we are baptized by one Spirit into one body, whether Jew or Gentile, whether slave or free, and we have all been made to drink of one Spirit. God has set each one of the members in the body just as He pleased. Though His Spirit is measured out individually to each of us, I believe we experience the fullness of His Spirit as one body working together in unity.

He gave some to be apostles, some prophets, some evangelists, some pastors and teachers, for the equipping of the saints for the work of ministry, for the edifying of the body of Christ, until we all come to the unity of the faith and the knowledge of the Son of God, to a perfect (mature) man, to the measure of the stature of the fullness of Christ; that we should no longer be children, tossed to and fro and carried about with ever wind of doctrine, by the trickery of men, in the cunning craftiness of deceitful plotting, but speaking the truth in love, may grow up in all things into Him who is the head Christ. The purpose of these appointments determined by Him is to teach us of Him and to build us in Him. He indicates that these selections and functions will continue until we as one body come into unity of faith and knowledge of the Son of God. Our maturity is only possible as the Holy Spirit of God functions through the men and women He has anointed with gifts and when His body responds through obedience to His Word. This will transform us into the glorious bride of Christ who is ready for her King.

The Holy Spirit is our teacher. His Word tells us concerning those who try to deceive or lead us astray that the Holy Spirit, which we have received from Him, abides within us. His Word says that we need no teacher because we have His Spirit; thus, we have the ability to discern what is the truth and what is a lie concerning all things. Our discernment is from Him, the Spirit of truth, who leads us into all truth.

God has given us the means and instruction that we are to walk in the Spirit. He tells us that in doing so we will not fulfill the lust of the flesh. He warns us that our flesh lusts against His Spirit and His Spirit against our flesh. They are contrary to one another. Through His Spirit, we have the ability to overcome every opposition. Furthermore, He has given us His armor, which is spiritual. For our battle is not with flesh and blood, but with principalities and powers of darkness. With the armor of God, we are able to withstand in the evil day. God is within His people empowering us to walk in His Spirit and in compliance with His Word.

God's Holy Spirit of wisdom gave us His Son as Savior. His Word became flesh and dwelt among us. He gave us His Spirit to teach, guide, keep, and seal us until the day of our redemption. By His Word and through His Spirit, we have every weapon, all knowledge, and the complete understanding we need to act in wisdom and strength in every situation. We have access to the very throne of God, and His Spirit helps us in our weaknesses. For we do not know what we should pray for as we ought, but the Holy Spirit Himself makes intercession for us with groanings that cannot be uttered. He who searches the hearts knows what the mind of the Spirit is because He makes intercessions for His saints according to the will of God. He is God, and Holy is His Name.

Chapter 7
To Know God: A Personal Journey

God in His infinite wisdom and knowledge has created a path for each of us. The path leads to holiness, communion, and ultimately a union or oneness with Him. The door to this path is Jesus Christ. Each of His sheep must come through the door of salvation to begin walking on the path. The beauty in this personal journey calls for some discussion. When anyone undertakes a journey, he or she plans the details of that voyage. Where am I going? How will I get there? What will the journey require in terms of time commitment or equipment? Who will be with me? Why am I going? The personal journey God created is beautiful because He has made every provision for us. He has designed the journey. He knows where we are going, how we will get there, and what the journey will require of us. He has given us His Spirit and Word to guide us. He will be with us, and He planned why it is necessary for us to take the journey. He is the author and the finisher of our faith.

The personal journey God created is beautiful. He has made every provision for us.

Each of us is wonderfully and fearfully made in the image of God. He knows every hair on our heads, and He knows the breadth and depth of our lives from the beginning of them to the end. He knows what path each of us will take, and only He can make our crooked paths straight. He knows all the detours and challenges we will encounter. God stated that He desires for all men (and women) to be saved and to come to the knowledge of Christ. He desires that His people everywhere would lift up holy hands in praise to Him. He desires that we have clean hands and pure hearts. He requires that we do justly, love mercy, and walk humbly before the Lord our God. He desires that we be perfect, even as our Father in heaven is perfect.

God has allowed us to be self-determined. The journey for each of us is specific and individually determined upon our own hearts, desires, faith, fears, obedience, and rebellions. As we sojourn through the path of life, the difficulty in our journey will be a result of our submission to God or lack thereof. The beauty in this journey is that God has made every provision for us to walk through it all to the end. In addition, He has promised that those who endure to the end will be saved.

God's grace is given to us to begin, endure, and complete our journey. God's grace is more than our minds can comprehend because it is a spiritual gift that cannot be seen or handled and is rarely taught in truth. God's grace is omnipresent, just as God is, and His grace is acknowledged by our faith. As defined by J. F. Strombeck, grace is the unmerited, abounding provision of the unrestrained operation of God's infinite love through Jesus Christ on behalf of humankind, especially those who depend on Him. Grace is God's love in action. By grace we are saved through faith and that not of ourselves; it is a gift from God, not of works, lest any man should boast. God's grace that allows us to be saved is the door that opens to the beginning of our journey.

Therefore, the journey begins. We receive God's gift of salvation given by grace through faith, and we walk through the door. Our journey begins with being born again: by confessing and receiving Jesus as Lord, which ultimately leads to eternal life with Him. Almost immediately after this initial point in the journey, many will falter, stumble, loiter, or perhaps quit for various reasons. On this personal journey, each of us must walk with God and before God in submission to Him. We walk with God because He is with us, and we walk before Him in submission because we are not equal to God. We do not walk alone. However, our obedience, commitment, disobedience, or sin is completely solitary. Each of us must walk before God with sincerity in our own hearts. Our journey cannot be without purpose of heart, but rather, it must be with the commitment of obedience and with servitude to our Lord and God as we walk circumspectly and deliberately. Those who falter or make a false start at the beginning of the journey should consider why they called upon His name in the first place. If it was truly from a repentant and expectant heart, then they should rise up and begin anew. If it was for any other reason, God will reveal that to them. His Word says the sower sowed the Word like seeds, but some fell by the wayside; it was trampled down, and the birds of the air devoured it. When He told this parable, Jesus revealed that those by the wayside are the ones who hear the Word, but then the devil comes and takes the Word out of their hearts, lest they should believe and be saved.

God is for us. He is our greatest advocate and truly our helper. Too often we look to other people and places to gain the help and understanding we need. It really does not matter how insurmountable the mountain is on our journey or how rugged the creek we must cross. God is greater than anything we encounter in life! We have the Wonderful Counselor and the Holy Spirit to help us and guide us in all truth. We must take an honest look at our hearts in light of the purity of His Word, and we must pray that He will allow us to see ourselves for what we truly are: miserable without Him. Then we need a sorrowful and repentant heart toward God for success in our journey with Him.

Our walk with God involves learning of Him and doing what He requires of us. We must desire to know God, and we must seek Him until we have found Him. We must know His Word to understand His ways, and then we must comprehend how we will gain eternal life in Him. The purpose of the journey is to know God. We persist on this journey by meditating on His Word and by seeking His will in prayer. We can find a place to gather with other believers and share in the Word of God, the praise of God, and in fellowship with one another. However, it is not the responsibility of the pastor or other Christians to walk our journey. That we must do for ourselves. It is not the responsibility of the pastor or others to remove all the stones from our path and make our path smooth. That is a task for us and our Maker. When we were babies, our mothers fed us. As we grew, we held our own bottles and cups. At some point, we picked up forks and spoons and fed ourselves. As we grew into adulthood, we chose our own food, prepared it, and consumed it. In the same manner, we must grow to maturity as we walk our personal journey with God.

There isn't a timetable or formula to determine the length of time of our personal journey with God. We in part determine our journey based upon our commitment and the decisions we make. He reveals Himself to us as we journey with Him. We must always remember that His riches are unsearchable. He said that if we seek Him, we will find Him. If we knock, He will answer. God is an ever-present source of power in our lives if we submit to His will. On our personal journey, we should be enlightened daily. As we journey on our path each day, we should learn from our missteps and stumbles as well as our sure footings and glories. On the journey, we should learn from the examples given throughout His Word of how God deals with His people, and we should expect Him to deal with us in the same manner. God is no respecter of persons and He does not change. Our path then indeed grows brighter and brighter.

Let's reflect on the journey of the Israelites in the Old Testament, who later became known as the Jews. God was their King, and He had given them the prophet Samuel to speak His Word to them, to guide them, and to judge them. As Samuel grew old, the people came together and demanded a king. They wanted to be like other nations in that this king would judge them and go before them and fight their battles for them. They wanted a king that they could see with their eyes, not just with their hearts. They failed to understand that God was the One who led them whether a man was on the throne or not. It was God who protected them and God who fought their battles and made all nations fear them because of His display of power and strength on behalf of His people. They forgot and forsook God. In His goodness, He warned them of what their king would do to them, and still they clamored for a king. Therefore, God gave them what they unwisely asked for. He allowed them to walk a crooked path. God allowed them to suffer the consequences of their ungrateful and foolish hearts and to suffer greatly on their journey.

The same heart resides in some of God's people today. Some who do not know God for themselves foolishly and sometimes rebelliously demand from God that which is not planned for their journey. God, who knows all things, knows that the thing that they clamor for will not lead them on the journey that He planned for them. Yet they cry louder until God allows them to have what they desire, and they suffer the consequences of their folly. Many suffer so much that they blame God and never return to the Lord. Others wander throughout their whole lives never knowing the goodness of God. Still others go through the motions and display self-righteousness, but they never enter the kingdom of God. Thus, they never enjoy the blessing of a personal journey with God.

God has a plan for His people—those who believe on Jesus as their Lord and Savior. He has determined our path. However, He will not force us to walk the journey He has chosen or provided. We must choose Him and let our journey unfold before us as we walk with Him continually. He has told us that He has set life and death before us, and we must choose life. Nevertheless, He will not force us. We learn that God requires that we walk uprightly before Him, and that in doing so, His light will shine in all the earth. God is a jealous God. When His people forget about Him and choose other gods and varying paths, He displays His displeasure by allowing them to become captive in bondage, or to be broken but not utterly destroyed. His hope is that they will turn from their wickedness and return their hearts unto Him.

We have been equipped for our journey with all that we need. However, too many believers do not understand the difference between trials and tribulation on this earth and the torment of sin and disobedience. This confusion causes many to quit their journey prematurely. There is a vast difference between the two. The Word tells us regarding tribulations that the godly will suffer because of Christ and His righteousness. This is persecution for Jesus's sake, and is not without reward. Regarding tribulation, His Word says that it produces endurance, which must be cultivated within us to continue on our journey and make it to the end. Regarding trials, the Bible says, "Beloved, do not think it strange concerning the fiery trial which is to try you as though some strange thing happened to you; but rejoice to the extent that you partake in Christ's sufferings, so that when His glory is revealed, you may also be glad with exceeding joy." Joy is not just a feeling; it is the deep sense of delightful confidence we feel deep within us when we know that the end of our trials are victories in Him. After we have endured trials and tribulations, our faith becomes stronger in Him and our stride increases. We mature in Him. He increases and we decrease.

We all endure everyday life circumstances that challenge us and test our faith. We cannot become perplexed and stumble because of them. God makes His sun to rise on the evil and on the good, and He sends rain on the just and on the unjust. No temptation has overtaken us except such as is common to man; but God is faithful, who will not allow us to be tempted beyond what we are able, but with the temptation will also make the way of escape, that we may be able to bear it. The way of escape is always through obedience to His Word. Because we live on the earth, we will encounter stress, pressure, and upsetting events, but that must not disrupt our journey. God has made every provision for us.

Let us never forget that sin brings us into bondage and leads to death. The bondage of sin is slavery to the very thing we have submitted ourselves to, and the outcome of sin is torment. The wrath of God comes on the sons of disobedience. When our personal desires take us away from His will, we find ourselves captive to the very thing that drew us away. The sin within us leads us away from the journey that is set before us. Sin and disobedience will only lead to death and destruction. Beloved, do not be deceived; no one that walks such a course in this life will attain eternal life.

The blessings in this journey with God are His peace, His righteousness, and His joy in His Spirit. Herein is the Kingdom of God. Where are we going on this journey, and why are we going there? We are journeying toward salvation with eternal life in God as our final destination and with our hearts filled with the expectation of holiness and the hope of godliness. With God's Spirit as our tutor on our journey and His Word as the lamp that lights our path, we forge ahead with confidence. All that is required of us on this journey is that we love Him with all our hearts, all our minds, and all our strength. He has given us the armor of God so that we may withstand. Jesus and His Father will make their abode in us. He did not leave us as orphans but sent us another comforter, His Holy Spirit, and He is in us. He will never forsake us, and He will be with us until the end.

This is Just the Beginning

After many years of insecurity, numerous re-write, having to purge oneself and always keeping the Word of God before her eyes, Adoria has completed her first work. I remember when the Lord breathed in our spirits and said "Breathed Ink". We did not quite know what that would entail, but our response was and always will be yes Lord.

The process of bringing forth this work, has been work in deed. I remember reviewing the first draft of the book and thinking "this is undecipherable." The hardest part was telling my dear friend, my sister, my confidant that the work missed the mark and needed to be rewritten. Today we celebrate the faithfulness and the goodness of God. His grace has brought us to this moment in time.

For I know the thoughts that I think toward you, says the Lord, thoughts of peace and not of evil, to give you a future and a hope.

Rita Zeigler

About the Author

Adoria Luster, called and anointed by God, began her ministry in 1987. God stood over her, called her name and told her to respond, "Here I am". She obeyed. In 1991 at a John Osteen convention the Spirit of the Lord poured oil on her head anointing her for His purpose. Adoria is devoted to the building and restoring of the church of God through teaching and preaching the Word of truth. Her ministry is committed to the revelation and demonstration that "we are the church", not in attending church.

She is the mother of three children, Jasmine, Precyous and Jeremiah. Her husband Donnie Luster is a gracious and strong supporter of all God has required of her.

www.ingramcontent.com/pod-product-compliance
Lightning Source LLC
Chambersburg PA
CBHW071733020426
42331CB00008B/2010